T0152132

MY FIVE-YEAR

RECOVERY PLANNER

LOOKING TO THE FUTURE,
ONE DAY AT A TIME

CENTRAL RECOVERY PRESS

CENTRAL RECOVERY PRESS

Central Recovery Press (CRP) is committed to publishing exceptional materials addressing addiction treatment, addiction recovery, and behavioral health care, including original and quality books, audio/visual communications, and Web-based new media. Through a diverse selection of titles, it seeks to impact the behavioral health care field with a broad range of unique resources for professionals, recovering individuals, their families, and the general public.

For more information, visit www.centralrecoverypress.com.

Central Recovery Press, Las Vegas, NV 89129
© 2010 by Central Recovery Press, Las Vegas, NV

ISBN-13: 978-0-9818482-9-7
ISBN-10: 0-9818482-9-X

All rights reserved. Published 2010. Printed in the United States of America.

No part of this publication may be reproduced, stored in a retrieval system, or transmitted in any form or by any means, electronic, mechanical, photocopying, recording, or otherwise, without the written permission of the publisher.

16 15 14 13 12 11 10   1 2 3 4 5

Publisher: Central Recovery Press
            3371 N Buffalo Drive
            Las Vegas, NV 89129

Cover design and interior by Sara Streifel, Think Creative Design

To the clients
and alumni
of Las Vegas
Recovery Center.

TABLE OF CONTENTS

The Planning Paradox of Twelve-Step Recovery

Recovery gives each of us the opportunity to be co-creators, along with our Higher Power, of a new and bright future for ourselves and our families.

The foundation of twelve-step recovery is not to use "just for today, one day at a time." Members are encouraged to stay in the now and to avoid getting caught up in making plans. We are taught to look back at—but not dwell on—our past in order to clean up our messes and make amends, but we are discouraged from making detailed plans for the future…aren't we? Yes and no.

Recovery teaches us that although we are not in control of outcomes, we are in control of our actions. We have choices today; we can do the next right thing and allow our Higher Power to be in charge of the results, instead of trying to assert our will over people, places, and things that we were never in control of to begin with. So although we know today that we don't control outcomes, we know that we control the things we do.

Our recovery programs teach us that our Higher Power will do for us what we cannot do for ourselves, implying that there is a great deal we can and must do for ourselves. This five-year recovery planner will help you clarify and chart the steps you need to take in order to create the future you want. It will help you reach for your dreams, even if you're not sure of what your dreams are right now.

We hope you enjoy playing in this simple little journal and take the steps needed to start (or continue) on the journey of a lifetime—your recovery.

The Editors of Central Recovery Press

The exercises in this journal are intended to appeal to seekers of all types—whether you are a writer, a list-maker, a poet, a photographer, a scrapbooker, or a sketch artist. You don't need to fill in every blank or complete every activity. This is YOUR five-year recovery planner, and the activities have been designed to appeal to your learning and growing style, no matter what it is.

INTRODUCTION

Dreams Call for Planning, Not for Controlling

You may hear these words or a variation of them in twelve-step meetings: "If I had made a list of what I wanted from life when I first entered recovery, I'd have sold myself short." When a person enters recovery, often all he or she wants is for the pain to stop, the obsession to quiet down, and the mess that has been made of life to be cleaned up. But once recovery has begun to take hold, and the recovering individual begins to work the steps with a sponsor, to be of service, and to attend meetings, the realization that there is more to life than just abstaining from active addiction begins to dawn. The possibility of living "a life beyond one's wildest dreams" now seems to be more than just a distant prospect. It begins to seem more like reality.

Think of all that addiction has robbed from you—perhaps you have lost your family, your home, your possessions, and your hope, along with your self-respect and self-esteem. Relationships may be dead or dying; friendships that were once vital may seem all but impossible to revive. Money problems may be a looming threat. Yet, you see others in your recovery fellowship beginning

This planner is not a Fourth- or Tenth-Step inventory guide. Rather than looking back at past mistakes and character defects you need to address, you will be identifying your wishes, hopes, and dreams for the future. You will lay out a vision of your future and discover for yourself the steps you need to take to make that future a reality. It's a beautiful thing to look forward to living life beyond your wildest dreams; but first, it's important to identify and clarify what those dreams really are. This journal can help.

to thrive. Since you now know the program of recovery that works for them works for you, perhaps you are allowing yourself to hope that you, too, can regain some of what you've lost and that you can rebuild a new and better life—and you can. But how?

Recovery teaches us to be grateful for what we have in our lives today, and no matter what, each of us can find something to be grateful for.

Making a five-year recovery plan calls on each of us to continue to build on the assets we have discovered as we worked the steps. These are worthwhile and acceptable activities that can help us build a stronger recovery.

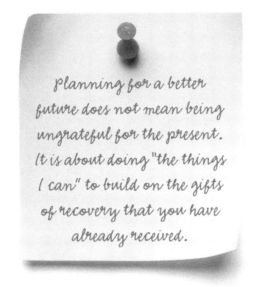

Planning for a better future does not mean being ungrateful for the present. It is about doing "the things I can" to build on the gifts of recovery that you have already received.

List the wildest dreams you have right now. Don't be too analytical or hypercritical. There's no right or wrong answer; think of this as a sort of "benchmark" for future reference.

_____

_____

_____

_____

_____

_____

_____

_____

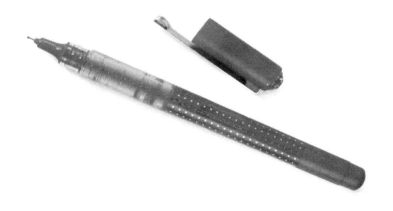

A BALANCING ACT

The Four Points of Balance

As human beings we are endowed with four aspects of our natures that can be categorized as the *physical, mental, emotional,* and *spiritual* parts of our existence. In recovery, we first begin to heal physically, as toxins are removed from our bodies. As our thoughts become clearer, we start to heal mentally. Emotional healing begins as the mask of addiction wears away and we begin to connect with our feelings again. Finally, we heal spiritually as we seek a connection with our Higher Power. This is not a prescribed, but rather a descriptive progression, based on the experiences of many people in recovery. Your progression may differ, but will likely include these four "recoveries" within your recovery.

Finding harmony and peace of mind in life is one of the goals of recovery.

As we seek to align these four points of balance, we build and maintain a strong foundation. While we will never master perfect balance, this is the ideal that we strive toward.

Too much focus on any one point will throw us out of kilter. For example, many of us enter recovery in terrible physical condition and wish to improve our health and fitness, which is a laudable goal. However, an overemphasis on physical exercise or extreme dieting, especially in early recovery, will leave little energy for attention to the mental, emotional, and spiritual aspects of our lives. Similarly, an overemphasis on spiritual development might impede our emotional growth if we focus too intently on prayer, meditation, worship, or other solitary spiritual practices to the detriment of our emotional lives with family and friends. Being overly emotional may tend to cloud our thoughtful, mental reactions to life events, and so on. This journal, which you will begin to create for yourself on the following pages, will help you focus equally on each of the four points of balance in your five-year recovery plan.

What does balance mean to you?

_____

_____

_____

_____

What actions can you take right now to help you find balance in your recovery and life?

_____

_____

_____

_____

What do you think your recovery and life will look like in five years?

_____

_____

_____

_____

_____

_____

_____

USING THE "SERENITY PRAYER" AS A RESOURCE

Members of twelve-step recovery fellowships are familiar with a short devotion known as the "Serenity Prayer." In its most common form, it asks a Higher Power to...

"...grant me the serenity to accept the things I cannot change,

The courage to change the things I can, and

The wisdom to know the difference."

In this form, it is attributed to German theologian Reinhold Neibuhr, although as he himself said, he may have encountered the prayer or some variant of it years earlier. It's true that there are many similar prayers found in many different traditions dating back to antiquity. It was introduced into twelve-step recovery by a member who had encountered it and found it helpful. The "Serenity Prayer" soon became one of the favorite prayers of persons in recovery and today is recited at many twelve-step meetings.

One solution to restore balance in your daily experience of life is to consciously separate what you may want from the reality of the situation. It's normal, natural, and understandable to want things the way you want them, but recovery requires an ability to accept the things you cannot change. Applying the "Serenity Prayer" and focusing consciously on identifying the things you cannot change, as well as what you can do to better accept those things, will make noticeable, positive, and healthy differences in your experience of life. It is essential to remember that one thing you can always change is how you respond to the people, events, and situations in your life.

You can incorporate the "Serenity Prayer" into your recovery and into the exercises in this five-year planner. People, places, and things—even some things about yourself—will not change for you. In some cases, you will need to change your reaction to them. In others, you need to simply accept them and move on to the best of your ability. Applying the "Serenity Prayer" as a tool to clarify the things you cannot change—and therefore need to find a way to accept—versus the things you can change, is a solution-oriented approach to achieving balance and strengthening your recovery. (Use extra pages if necessary; don't be limited to writing in the blank spaces provided.)

Applying the "Serenity Prayer"

"...grant me the serenity to accept the things I cannot change,

The courage to change the things I can, and

The wisdom to know the difference."

Related to your current life, identify something you cannot change and need to accept.

_____

_____

_____

_____

_____

Describe how you will begin to go about accepting it.

_____

_____

_____

_____

Related to your current life, identify something you can change.

_____

_____

_____

_____

_____

Describe how you will begin to go about changing it.

_____

_____

_____

_____

_____

Describe how you can tell the difference between what you can and cannot change.

_____

_____

_____

_____

_____

In each of the following sections of this book, you will have an opportunity to use the Serenity Prayer as a resource for planning your future.

Thoughts:

MY PHYSICAL FUTURE

People often underestimate or deny the importance of their physical state to the quality of their lives, but the reality is that it is impossible to separate your physical condition from your overall state of balance. The four points of balance are inextricably connected. In other words, your body, mind, emotions, and spirit are constantly affecting each other. Each of us is here on earth in a physical body, and how we take care of our bodies directly affects how we think and feel about everything.

What are the recognizable signs of physical balance? Are they expressed in a "perfect" face, physique, hair color, or smile? Is a person in physical balance a marathon runner or tri-athlete? Maybe, but not necessarily. Although each person on earth has much in common with every other person, each of our bodies has different needs and abilities.

We know that we need fresh air, clean water, wholesome food, adequate sleep, and a certain amount of exercise in order to maintain our physical well-being. Some of us are happier with an athletic life that includes regular, vigorous exercise. Others are happier in a lifestyle that may be less active, but still allows for the performance of daily activities. Still others have physical lives that are defined by chronic pain or other physical challenges. Yet, no matter what physical type we are—active, sedentary, or challenged—there is an optimal physical state for each of us.

Whatever your optimal state is, working toward physical balance requires doing things each day to take care of and strengthen your body. Some common characteristics of physical balance include

- Eating nutritious foods
- Exercising regularly
- Avoiding toxins
- Getting enough sleep
- Practicing relaxation
- Practicing meditation

Listen to your body; it is always giving you clues about what it needs to be healthy. Paying attention to these subtle signals is a powerful way to improve your physical balance.

When we neglect ourselves physically, we don't have the energy and vitality to excel in the other areas. How can you be your best if you're taxing your body with poor nutrition, lack of exercise, inadequate sleep, excessive toxins, and unmanaged stress? Without physical balance, it will be difficult to live a life you love.

One of the most common reasons people give for not attending to their physical needs is a lack of time. Overcoming this obstacle simply requires applying some problem-solving skills to make it a part of each day. By bringing awareness to your daily habits and routines, you are taking the first step toward meaningful change. And remember that a positive change, even a small one, in one point of balance tends to produce positive changes in all the others.

Start laying the foundation for your optimal physical state, beginning with acceptance of wherever you are right now, and acknowledgment of what you can and cannot change.

My Physical Plan: Warming Up

You can begin to strengthen your foundation by examining where you are now and how you feel about it, then looking at some goals you would like to achieve. You can think of this as the "warm-up phase" of your physical balance journey.

Begin where you are. Check off each item based on how you feel about it today. Use the blank boxes to add any physical concerns you have that are not listed.

CHECK ONE:	(DISLIKE)	(OKAY)	(LIKE)
My Overall Health			
Diet			
Fitness			
Strength			
Flexibility			
Endurance			
Body Type			
Energy			
Weight			
Skin			
Teeth			
Hair			

My Five-Year Plan Goals

Your goals can be simple or lofty, as long as they are your goals and no one else's.

Five years from now I'd like (fill in the blank next to the physical item listed.)

My Overall Health to Be _____

My Diet to Be _____

My Fitness to Be _____

My Strength to Be _____

My Flexibility to Be _____

My Endurance to Be _____

My Body Type to Be _____

My Energy to Be _____

My Weight to Be _____

My Skin to Be _____

My Teeth to Be _____

My Hair to Be _____

My _____ to Be _____

My _____ to Be _____

My _____ to Be _____

If you're not happy with your physical life today, what would you like to change or improve?

_____

_____

_____

_____

_____

Whether or not you are happy with your physical state today, please list the **top five** things you would like to either change or maintain about your physical existence as it is today.

1. _____

2. _____

3. _____

4. _____

5. _____

What can you do today to start to change or to maintain those five items?

Item	What I Can Do Today to Achieve the Goal I Want in Five Years

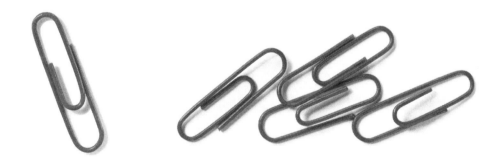

Your physical being can include your physical and material life (i.e., what you have, your external possessions) circumstances. Are you happy with your physical life today? If so, why? (Use the spaces below.) Remember, recovery teaches us to be grateful for what we have today. This exercise is not about being ungrateful; rather it is about examining the aspects of your physical life that may be within your control to build on and improve.

_____

_____

_____

_____

Continue with your material life circumstances. Are you happy with your material life today? If so, why? (Use the spaces below.)

_____

_____

_____

_____

My Nutrition Condition

Much like a car needs fuel to run, your body needs the energy provided by the foods you eat in order to function. And the higher the quality of "fuel" you give your body, the better it will run, and the better your overall health and wellness will be. Good nutrition involves consuming the right balance of carbohydrates, proteins, and fats, along with essential vitamins and minerals. As you begin to set your nutritional goals, you may want to build your knowledge about healthy eating and bring more awareness to your food choices (where your food comes from, how it is produced, how certain foods make you feel, etc.), then incorporate this information into your plan.

Thoughts:

Begin where you are. Check off each item based on how you feel about it today.

CHECK ONE:	(DISLIKE)	(OKAY)	(LIKE)
My Eating Habits			
My Sugar Intake			
My Fat Intake			
My Vegetable Intake			
My Fruit Intake			
My Protein Intake			
My Carbohydrate Intake			
My Animal Products Intake (Meat, Dairy, Eggs)			
My Vitamin/Supplement Intake			
My Water Intake			
My Salt Intake			
My Processed Foods Intake			

My Five-Year Plan Goals

Five years from now I'd like (fill in the blank next to the nutrition item listed.)

My Eating Habits to Be _____

My Sugar Intake to Be _____

My Fat Intake to Be _____

My Vegetable Intake to Be _____

My Fruit Intake to Be_____

My Protein Intake to Be _____

My Carbohydrate Intake to Be _____

My Animal Products Intake to Be_____

My Vitamin/Supplement Intake to Be _____

My Water Intake to Be _____

My Salt Intake to Be_____

My Processed Foods Intake to Be _____

My _____ to Be _____

My _____ to Be _____

My _____ to Be _____

How I Will Achieve My Nutrition Goals

Now write specific actions you can begin to do to implement the changes you listed.

Within 3 – 6 Months I Will _____

_____

I'm Doing This Because _____

_____

Within 1 – 2 Years I Will _____

_____

I'm Doing This Because _____

_____

Within 3 – 4 Years I Will _____

_____

I'm Doing This Because _____

_____

Write, draw, or cut and paste pictures as indicated below.

My Favorite Foods

My Favorite Places to Eat

My Favorite Recipe (Paste or write in the space provided.)

In the next five years I would like to eat at

Five years from now, if a restaurant named a dish after me, it would be called

_____

_____

_____

_____

_____

Five years from now I would like to be eating

Less of This	More of This

Focus on Fitness

A good workout can do wonders for your body, mind, and spirit. By incorporating at least a moderate amount of exercise into your daily life (thirty minutes, three to six times a week), you can experience a wide range of benefits, including a stronger heart, increased energy and alertness, lower stress levels, less anxiety and depression, lower risk of disease, increased self-esteem, and better performance of everyday activities. It doesn't really matter what type of exercise you do, but if you do something you enjoy, you'll be much more likely to keep doing it. Also, setting specific and measurable goals can help you stay motivated to keep moving.

My Five-Year Plan Goals

List five fitness goals you would like to achieve in the next five years.

1. _____

2. _____

3. _____

4. _____

5. _____

What can you do today to start working toward those goals?

Item	What I Can Do Today to Achieve the Goal I Want in Five Years

How I Will Achieve My Fitness Goals

Now write specific things you can do to implement the changes you listed.

Within 3 – 6 Months I Will _____

_____

I'm Doing This Because _____

_____

Within 1 – 2 Years I Will _____

_____

I'm Doing This Because _____

_____

Within 3 – 4 Years I Will _____

_____

I'm Doing This Because _____

_____

Create a visual representation as indicated below. You can draw, cut out pictures (magazines and catalogs are good sources), or use your own photos.

My favorite workout clothes	My favorite workout/exercise shoes
My favorite types of exercise	**My favorite place to work out/exercise**

Take a Look at Toxins

A toxin is a poison that can affect any part or system of the body, internally or externally. Drugs, including the drug alcohol, when used excessively or for purposes other than those prescribed to treat a medical condition, are classified as toxins. Toxins can be natural or man-made.

Toxins can enter the body through food, water, air, or physical contact with the skin or mucous membranes. They can also be produced inside the body through normal metabolic processes or through the decomposition of foods in the small and large intestines. Under normal circumstances, the body is able to eliminate toxins from the body via urine, feces, exhalation, and perspiration. Thus, the major organs involved in elimination are the kidneys, liver, colon, lungs, and skin.

The liver is the organ primarily responsible for breaking toxins into harmless byproducts, which are eliminated in the feces or through the kidneys into the urine. Often, in persons who have abused drugs, including the drug alcohol, these organs of elimination have been stressed.

Thoughts:

Toxins I Take in

Take a look at some of the common toxins listed in the column on the left and put a check in the appropriate box to indicate whether or not you currently use it.

TOXIN	YES	NO	DON'T KNOW
Nicotine			
Refined Sugar			
Saturated Fats			
Chlorine			
Acetone (Nail Polish Remover)			
Aluminum (Deodorant/ Antiperspirant)			
Benzene (Detergents, Pesticides, Adhesives)			
Sodium Chloride (Table Salt)			
Toluene (Nail Polish and Cleaning Products)			
Food Preservatives (Sulfites, MSG, Pesticides, etc.)			
Artificial Sweeteners (Aspartame, Saccharine, etc.)			

Ta-Ta to Toxins

If you are concerned about some of the toxins listed (or any others), use the space below to plan ways to decrease and/or eliminate them from your everyday life over the next five years. What is your five-year goal with regard to toxins?

_____

_____

_____

_____

_____

_____

_____

_____

_____

_____

_____

_____

Snooze Support

Sleep is one of our most important life-sustaining activities. Sleep is as important a survival need as food, water, or shelter; however, too many people do not get enough sleep for a number of reasons.

- **Life commitments**: Today's busy schedules seem to have everyone "burning the candle at both ends."

- **Attitude**: Too often sleep is looked upon as a want rather than a need.

- **Poor sleep habits (sometimes referred to as *sleep hygiene*)**: Sleeping in front of the TV or on the couch may seem restful, but truly restful sleep may require changing your sleeping conditions. The amount of light, noise, the surface you sleep on, and the ambient temperature all play a part in restful sleep.

- **Dietary factors**: Many of us don't realize that foods and other substances we ingest may play a part in determining how much or how little we sleep, as well as affecting the quality of our sleep.

- **Effects of exercise**: Regular exercise during the day helps people sleep better at night; however, timing is everything. Physical exercise too close to bedtime keeps some people awake. The body may need a chance to wind down after exercise.

My Sleeping Solutions

Begin where you are. How did you sleep last night?

_____

_____

_____

_____

_____

Are you happy with the quality and the quantity of your sleep in general? Why or why not?

_____

_____

_____

_____

_____

Do you want to change/improve the quality or quantity of your sleep? Beginning tonight, what changes might you make to improve the quality or quantity of your sleep?

_____

_____

_____

_____

_____

Five years from now, what changes would you like to see in your sleeping patterns?

_____

_____

_____

_____

_____

What will you do now to make those changes a reality?

_____

_____

_____

_____

_____

Do You Dig Your Digs?

Your home is part of your physical environment and an important element of your life. Describe your current living space, and you will probably find the description also reflects the condition of your life. So let's think about it.

Begin where you are. Check off each item based on how you feel about it today.

CHECK ONE:	(DISLIKE)	(OKAY)	(LIKE)
Overall Feel			
Layout			
Amount of Space			
Storage/Closet Space			
Natural Light			
Wall Color/Treatment			
Flooring			
Comfort			
Furniture			
Windows			
Privacy			
Neighborhood			
Cleanliness/Neatness			
Security			
Outside Noise/Light			

My Five-Year Plan Goals

Five years from now I'd like (fill in the blank next to the physical item listed.)

Overall Feel to Be _____

Layout to Be _____

Amount of Space to Be _____

Storage/Closet Space to Be _____

Natural Light to Be _____

Wall Color/Treatment to Be _____

Flooring to Be _____

Comfort to Be _____

Furniture to Be _____

Windows to Be _____

Privacy to Be _____

Neighborhood to Be _____

Cleanliness/Neatness to Be _____

Security to Be _____

Outside Noise/Light to Be _____

_____

_____

Mind Mapping for Physical Balance

Look at the map below. Indicate on the map the "places" you'd like to include in your physical five-year goals. Think of it as a plan for the world's greatest road trip. (Feel free to add new destinations of your own if the ones you want for yourself aren't here.)

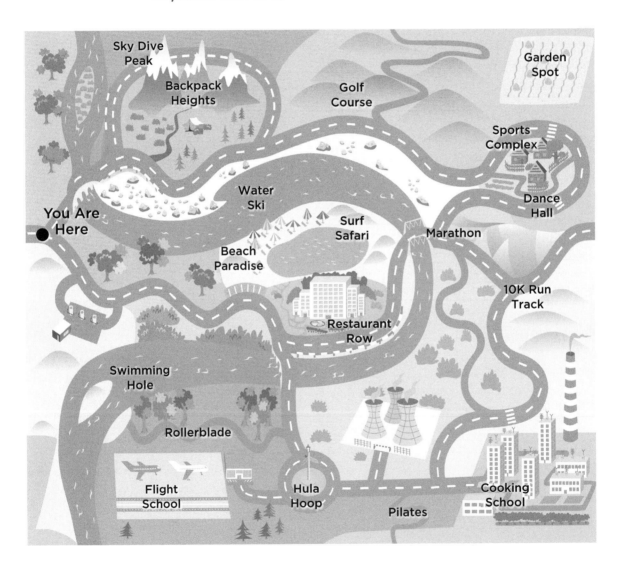

The Future File

Use these pages to record the beginning of your journey to your physical future. For example, if you decide to get a checkup, record your lab results here. If you're beginning a diet, start by recording your beginning weight and Body Mass Index (BMI). If you are planning on some wardrobe changes, take a photo of yourself today and paste it here…and maybe leave room for photos of your new look as your plan progresses. Getting a tattoo? Sketch the design here! Want a new haircut? Record your "before" look here…and maybe leave room for the "after" shot, as well. Whatever aspects of your physical experience you plan to devote your attention to, record them here, in whatever media you want—you can write, sketch, or enter this baseline data in any other way you want: It's YOUR future.

Putting It All Together

Look at what you like about your physical life today, and what you've discovered about your wishes, hopes, and dreams for the future. Use these pages to create a story, a poem, an essay, song lyrics, or list describing in words what your physical future will be like five years from now.

_____

_____

_____

_____

_____

_____

_____

_____

_____

_____

_____

_____

_____

_____

_____

_____

_____

_____

_____

_____

_____

_____

_____

_____

_____

_____

_____

_____

_____

_____

_____

_____

_____

_____

_____

_____

_____

_____

_____

_____

_____

How I Will Achieve My Physical Goals

Now write specific actions you can begin to do to implement the changes you listed.

Within 3 – 6 Months I Will _____

_____

I'm Doing This Because _____

_____

Within 1 – 2 Years I Will _____

_____

I'm Doing This Because _____

_____

Within 3 – 4 Years I Will _____

_____

I'm Doing This Because _____

_____

Applying the Serenity Prayer

"...grant me the serenity to accept the things I cannot change,

The courage to change the things I can, and

The wisdom to know the difference."

Related to your physical experience, identify something you cannot change and need to accept.

_____

_____

_____

_____

_____

Describe how you will begin to go about accepting it.

_____

_____

_____

_____

_____

Related to your physical experience, identify something you can change.

_____

_____

_____

_____

_____

Describe how you will begin to go about changing it.

_____

_____

_____

_____

Describe how you can tell the difference between what you can and cannot change.

_____

_____

_____

_____

The Big Picture

Using whatever technique you prefer (pen/pencil, marker, paints, photos you take yourself or cut from catalogs and magazines—or even a mixed-media combination of all of these), create the portrait of your physical future here.

MY MENTAL FUTURE

Mental fitness means different things to different people. Many consider the pursuit of formal education to be important, while others find intellectual fulfillment in reading or study undertaken on their own. Some people enjoy hobbies and sports, and feel sufficiently challenged and engaged. Others commit to pursuits such as reading or attending lectures. Some visit art museums or watch science-themed television shows, because those activities feed their mental lives. Others may make an effort to surround themselves with uplifting companions who add value to conversations and who always seem excited to share some new idea. There are many ways to achieve and maintain a healthy mental life. No matter where we begin or what our gifts or limitations are, there is an optimal mental state for each of us.

How would you describe your optimal mental state?

_____

_____

_____

_____

_____

Where are you now as compared with where you want to be mentally?

_____

_____

_____

_____

_____

Is there anything in your mental life that you wish you could change but haven't yet?

_____

_____

_____

_____

_____

My Mental Plan: Warming Up

Review the items below and place a check in the column that best describes how you feel. There are no right or wrong answers to this exercise.

Check off each item based on how you feel about it today.

CHECK ONE:	(DISLIKE)	(OKAY)	(LIKE)
My Education Level			
My Language Skills			
My Reading Ability			
My Reading Comprehension			
My Vocabulary			
My Conversation Skills			
My Memory			
My Observation Skills			
My Awareness of Current Events			
My Interest in Current Events			
My Reading Materials			
Books			
Newspapers			
Magazines			
Internet			
My Cultural Appreciation			
My Music Appreciation			
My Art Appreciation			

continued on page 58

CHECK ONE:	(DISLIKE)	(OKAY)	(LIKE)
My TV Viewing			
My Writing Skills			
My Math Skills			
My Science Knowledge			
My Life Skills			
My Cooking Ability			
The Way I Take Care of My Possessions			
My Housekeeping			
My Conversational Skills			
My Listening Skills			
My Time Management			
My Finances			
My Job Performance			
My Work Habits (e.g., punctuality)			
My Flexibility/Open-Mindedness			
My Responsibility			
My Willingness to Learn			

My Five-Year Plan Goals

When it comes to something as abstract as mental goal-setting, it can be difficult to articulate just what you want. This exercise may help you clarify and focus on your goals for your mental future.

Five years from now, I'd like (fill in the blank next to the mental item listed.)

My Education Level to Be _____

My Language Skills to Be _____

My Reading Ability to Be _____

My Reading Comprehension to Be_____

My Vocabulary to Be _____

My Conversation Skills to Be _____

My Memory to Be _____

My Observation Skills to Be _____

My Awareness of Current Events to Be _____

My Interest in Current Events to Be _____

My Reading Materials to Be _____

Books_____

Newspapers _____

Magazines _____

Internet _____

My Cultural Appreciation to Be _____

My Music Appreciation to Be_____

continued on page 60

My Art Appreciation to Be _____

My TV Viewing to Be _____

My Writing Skills to Be _____

My Math Skills to Be _____

My Science Knowledge to Be _____

My Life Skills to Be _____

My Cooking Ability to Be _____

The Way I Take Care of My Possessions to Be _____

My Housekeeping to Be _____

My Conversational Skills to Be _____

My Listening Skills to Be _____

My Time Management to Be _____

My Finances to Be _____

My Job Performance to Be _____

My Work Habits to Be _____

My Flexibility/Open-Mindedness to Be _____

My Responsibility to Be _____

My Willingness to Learn to Be _____

Whether or not you are happy with your mental state today, please list the **top five** things you would like to either change or maintain about your mental existence as it is today.

1. _____

2. _____

3. _____

4. _____

5. _____

What can you do today to start changing or to maintain those five items?

Item	What I Can Do Today to Achieve the Goal I Want in Five Years

Thought-Life or Inner Life

Your mental being includes your thought-life or inner life. Are your thoughts frequently along the lines of "What's for dinner?" Or do you often ask yourself questions like, "What is the meaning of life?"—or are your thoughts somewhere in-between? Neither kind of thought is better than the other, but they are decidedly different kinds of thoughts. The kinds of things you daydream, ponder over, and wonder about may tell you the kind of inner life or thought-life you have.

What kinds of things do you wonder about?

_____

_____

_____

_____

_____

Are you content with your thought-life today? If so, why are you content?

_____

_____

_____

_____

_____

_____

_____

Would you like to think differently about life—more deeply or philosophically? Or do you feel you are already too much of a "dreamer" who would like to be more down-to-earth? Which way do you feel, and why?

_____

_____

_____

_____

What would you like to change, maintain, or improve?

_____

_____

_____

_____

_____

_____

_____

Defining Myself without Limiting Myself

How many times have you said, "I'm the kind of person who…this," or "I'm not the kind of person who…that?" Do you set mental limitations on yourself by defining yourself in terms of your job, possessions, title, relationship status, etc.? Do your self-imposed limits restrict the kinds of activities you participate in, the kinds of foods you try, or the kind of music you listen to, and so on?

Do you stop yourself from trying new things because you think, "I'm not the sort of person who'd do that?" You might want to start defining yourself mentally now, in order to see just the sort of person you are today, before working on the sort of person you'd like to become. We can call this stock-taking your mental inventory (remember, this is not the same as a Fourth or Tenth Step inventory). Identify and examine whatever self-imposed mental limitations contribute to your mental state today.

Thoughts:

Just Who Do You Think You Are?

Take a moment to think about how you'd answer these questions today. Put a check in the column that best describes your attitude toward the activity in the center column, and use the blank center spaces to add some activities or beliefs of your own.

I'D ALWAYS…	ACTIVITY	I'D NEVER…
	Vote a Straight Party Ticket	
	Vote Independent	
	Plan My Day Like a To-Do List	
	Just "Go with the Flow"	
	Date a Person with Children	
	Match My Shoes to My Belt	
	Attend Religious Services	
	Say "Whatever You'd Like to Do" When My Partner Asks What I'd Like to Do	
	Sleep on the Same Side of the Bed	
	Recycle	

Never Say Never? Or Always and Forever?

Select three items from the list that you classified as "always," which you might like to change, and do the same for "never." Write down some ideas for how you will do that in the next five years, starting now.

I'll Change This "Always" to:_____

_____

I'll Change This "Always" to:_____

_____

I'll Change This "Always" to:_____

_____

I'll Change This "Never" to:_____

_____

I'll Change This "Never" to:_____

_____

I'll Change This "Never" to:_____

_____

What Do You Know?

We all have areas of expertise—things we feel comfortable and confident about doing. Then we have our wishes, hopes, and dreams—the things we've always wanted to learn about, do, see, or experience. These dreams may become reality as you make them part of your five-year recovery plan.

Look at the following chart. In the first column, write the activities and interests you feel comfortable doing now or that you take part in regularly. In the second column, write down all the activities you've thought about enjoying but just haven't yet tried, for whatever reason. In the third column, pick a few of the column two activities and write down what you plan to do about them in the next five years.

The exercises that follow are designed to allow you to see where you're at today, so that when you decide to broaden your mental horizons, you have an idea of where you've come from as you make plans to go where you want to go in the next five years.

I'M COMFORTABLE DOING	I'VE THOUGHT ABOUT DOING	I PLAN TO TRY

...A Few of My Favorite Things...

Do you have a favorite poem? Copy it here. (Look at this page in a few years, to see if it's still your favorite.)

_____

_____

_____

_____

_____

_____

_____

_____

_____

_____

_____

_____

_____

_____

_____

_____

Do you have favorite song lyrics? Use this space to record some favorite song lyrics that mean something to you today. (Over the next few years, look back at this page and see if they still mean the same thing.)

_____

_____

_____

_____

_____

_____

_____

_____

_____

_____

_____

_____

_____

_____

_____

_____

_____

_____

_____

If you were a poet, what would your poetry be about? Write your own poem, describing yourself at the beginning of your journey.

_____

_____

_____

_____

_____

_____

_____

_____

_____

_____

_____

_____

_____

_____

_____

_____

_____

What's the name of your favorite short story?

_____

_____

Write your own short story, to tell yourself where you are today and where you want to go on your journey of recovery.

_____

_____

_____

_____

_____

_____

_____

_____

_____

_____

_____

Do you have a favorite quote? Write it below, and explain what it means to you today.

_____

_____

_____

_____

_____

_____

_____

If someone were to quote you, what would you want them to say? What would you want your "famous last words" to be?

_____

_____

_____

_____

_____

_____

_____

What would you want your legacy of recovery to be?

_____

_____

_____

_____

_____

_____

_____

_____

_____

_____

_____

_____

_____

_____

_____

_____

Souvenirs to Save

As you embark on your journey to meet your mental future, be sure to bring back some souvenirs. Use these pages to collect and display the memorabilia you bring back from your "mental field trips," such as ticket stubs from a dance or theatre performance, postcards from museum gift shops, sheet music, photographs you take or print yourself; whatever mementos you collect as you stretch your mental horizons.

Putting It All Together

Look at what you like about your mental life today, and what you've discovered about your wishes, hopes, and dreams for the future. Use these pages to create a story, a poem, an essay, song lyrics, or list describing in words what your mental future will be like five years from now.

_____

_____

_____

_____

_____

_____

_____

_____

_____

_____

_____

_____

_____

_____

_____

_____

_____

_____

_____

_____

_____

_____

_____

_____

_____

_____

Applying the Serenity Prayer

"...grant me the serenity to accept the things I cannot change,

The courage to change the things I can, and

The wisdom to know the difference."

Related to your mental experience, identify something you cannot change and need to accept.

_____

_____

_____

_____

_____

Describe how you will begin to go about accepting it.

_____

_____

_____

_____

_____

Related to your mental experience, identify something you can change.

_____

_____

_____

_____

_____

Describe how you will begin to go about changing it.

_____

_____

_____

_____

Describe how you can tell the difference between what you can and cannot change.

_____

_____

_____

_____

_____

The Big Picture

Using whatever technique you prefer (pen/pencil, marker, paints, photos you take yourself or cut from catalogs and magazines—or even a mixed-media combination of all of these), create the portrait of your mental future here.

MY EMOTIONAL FUTURE

In recovery, emotional healing begins as the mask of addiction wears away and we begin to connect with our feelings again.

The focus of this section is how you can begin to create an emotionally balanced future for your life in recovery—to move, one day at a time—toward the emotional future you want for yourself. For example, by finding enjoyable activities that you can participate in and setting attainable goals, you can shift your attention toward hopefulness, gratitude, potential solutions, and taking action.

Creating a future where you experience emotional balance will involve many ingredients, but some are fundamental. These include: to learn and practice ways to become consciously aware of your feelings; to identify and express your feelings; to deal with distressing, uncomfortable feelings in healthier ways; and to strengthen positive feelings to promote your growing, healing, and recovery.

Emotional Balance

With emotional balance, you can accept your emotions, understanding that it's okay to feel whatever you are feeling. You pay close attention to your inner voice and are not held captive by the opinions and beliefs of others. You can identify your feelings and recognize that, although they are a part of you, they are NOT you. Noticing and accepting your feelings is therefore an important part of self-acceptance. This does not mean you wish to stay as you are, but when you first see and accept who you are (including your emotional experience) in the present moment, it allows you to make positive changes in your life.

You can start laying the foundation for your optimal emotional future by looking at where you are currently, and by identifying some of the goals you would like to achieve. Keep in mind that you are where you feel you are and not where you think you are.

My Emotional Plan: Warming Up

Place a check in the box that most accurately describes your level of satisfaction with how you handle each type of feeling—not just at this moment, but in general at this point in your life.

CHECK ONE:	(DISLIKE)	(OKAY)	(LIKE)
Fear			
Anxiety			
Anger			
Resentment			
Depression			
Sadness			
Grief/Loss			
Guilt			
Shame			
Serenity			
Love			
Happiness/Joy			
Gratitude			
Compassion/Empathy			

Developing an Emotional Vocabulary

Emotions/feelings are often talked about as if everyone knows what they are. However, this is not necessarily true. Many people are at least a little confused or uncertain about what is meant when specific feelings are discussed. For anyone who can benefit from clarification of what different feelings are, we offer the following brief descriptions.

Fear

Fear is the emotion of feeling afraid or extremely apprehensive. Fear often keeps its sufferers frozen in place, unable to move forward. Fear can also feed on itself in a dynamic wherein the more fearful you are, the more fearful you become, and the less able to function you are likely to be.

Anxiety

Anxiety is low-level fear. It is a distressing uneasiness, nervousness, or worry felt in response to any situation you anticipate to be threatening, and is usually accompanied by self-doubt about your capacity to cope with it.

Anger

Anger is an emotional response to things that don't go the way people want them to. It usually results from the experience of feeling "wronged" in some way. Problems with anger occur in how this powerful feeling is expressed, along a range from suppressing it—that is, keeping it inside—all the way to exploding.

Resentments

Resentments are related to anger in that they are negative feelings or ill will directed at someone or something experienced as "wrong," unjust, insulting, or disrespectful. Anger is about the present, whereas resentments relate to the past. They are a re-experiencing of past events and the old feelings of anger connected to them.

Depression, Sadness, Grief, and Loss

The feeling states of sadness, grief, and loss are closely related to one another and often fall underneath the umbrella of depression.

- Sadness refers to a feeling of unhappiness, while grief consists of distress related to the process of mourning a loss of some sort.

- Depression can be a feeling but also a mood—a more enduring emotional condition that exists on a continuum from mild to severe.

- Grief is a natural state of mourning attached to the loss of something.

- Loss occurs when someone or something is no longer available to us due to death, injury/illness or other health reasons, the end of a relationship, etc.

Shame and Guilt

Guilt is an emotion wherein we feel that we've *made* a mistake. It is defined as a feeling of having committed some wrong or failed in an obligation.

Shame, on the other hand, is an emotion where the feeling is that we *are* a mistake. Shame is defined as a painful feeling of humiliation or distress that is attached to how we perceive ourselves internally.

Serenity

Serenity is the state of being free from emotional or other upset or agitation.

Love

Love is the unselfish, benevolent affection, caring and concern for others.

Happiness

Happiness is a state of well-being and contentment.

Joy

Feelings of joy can occur from positive, pleasurable, or enjoyable experiences.

Gratitude

Gratitude is the state of being grateful; thankfulness.

Compassion

Compassion is the empathic awareness of others' distress, together with a desire to alleviate it.

Empathy

Empathy means to connect emotionally with others. It is understanding, being aware of and sensitive to, the feelings, thoughts, and experiences of another.

What Do Your Emotions Look Like?

For each of the emotions listed, find or create a visual representation of what it looks like for you. You can draw a picture or take one from a magazine, the Internet, etc.

Fear _____

Anxiety _____

Anger_____

Resentment _____

Depression, Sadness, Grief, and Loss _____

Shame and Guilt_____

Serenity _____

Love _____

Happiness _____

Joy _____

Gratitude_____

Compassion _____

Empathy _____

Other Emotions _____

Identifying, Feeling, and Expressing Emotions

The capacity to identify, feel, and express emotions is essential to overall health, well-being, and recovery. Yet, many people have great challenges with regard to identifying feelings and expressing them in ways that support emotional balance in their lives.

There are several levels of awareness and action involved in cultivating emotional balance:

1. The first level is becoming consciously aware that we are experiencing a feeling. This occurs when we first think about it or realize we feel something at that moment. Although we may not know specifically what the feeling is, it is important to simply notice and acknowledge that we have *some* feeling.

2. The next step is identifying what the particular feeling is. An important part of identifying your emotions is to put them into words. As an alternative to experiencing an undifferentiated mass of feelings, it is helpful to say to yourself, "I feel anxious," or "I feel angry," "I feel depressed," or "I feel serene," etc.

3. The more specific you can be in identifying your feelings, the more clear your understanding of your emotional experience will be. Moreover, identifying your feelings accurately enhances your ability to take the action(s) that are the best fit for your needs and support your recovery.

Connecting Emotions to Bodily Sensations

The following exercise will help you take the first steps toward increasing your emotional awareness and skills—knowing that feelings are present, what the feelings are, and how your feelings are connected to physical sensations in your body.

Learning how different emotions feel in your body in terms of their location (where you feel them) and sensation (what they feel like) will enable you to identify them more quickly and accurately. Read through the list of feelings in the left column and circle the ones you are experiencing. Next, take a moment to think about the sensation—it may be helpful to close your eyes and really turn your focus inward—then in the right column indicate where you experience each feeling *in your body*. For example, anger might be felt as tightness in your shoulders, sadness as an aching in your chest, fear as a knot in your stomach, and joy as warmth in your heart.

FEELING/EMOTION	WHERE AND HOW YOU FEEL IT IN YOUR BODY
Anger/Resentment	
Fear/Anxiety	
Depression/Sadness	
Grief/Loss	
Guilt/Shame	
Serenity	
Love	
Happiness/Joy	
Gratitude	
Compassion/Empathy	

Genuine acceptance of your feelings gives you the opportunity to shift your energy to thoughts and actions that facilitate the learning, growing, and healing that can fuel the continuing progress of your recovery.

Accepting Emotions Is Essential to Self-Acceptance

Sometimes you may think that you shouldn't feel the way you do. Feelings are neither good nor bad—they simply *are*. In the midst of intense negative feelings—whether fear, anger, depression, or whatever form your feeling may take—it can feel as though the feeling will last forever and like it will never end. To promote emotional balance, you can maintain an awareness that all feelings are temporary, and that they will *always* change!

Emotional balance is achieved when we allow ourselves to feel whatever comes up, and learn to accept our feelings without judging them. Because your feelings are a part of you, accepting them as they are is an important part of accepting yourself as you are.

For me, love means _____

_____

_____

_____

My greatest source of happiness/joy is _____

_____

_____

_____

It really touches my heart when _____

_____

_____

_____

I feel most at peace when _____

_____

_____

_____

I have the most compassion when _____

_____

_____

_____

The people I feel closest to are_____

_____

_____

_____

I feel closest to them because _____

_____

_____

_____

The things I appreciate most are _____

_____

_____

_____

I feel grateful when _____

_____

_____

_____

_____

_____

My Five-Year Plan Goals

Now it's time to choose some emotional goals. The goals you choose are for you and you alone. Simply allow yourself to imagine the emotional future you would like for yourself and write.

List the **top five** things you would like to either change or maintain about your emotional life as it is today.

1. _____

2. _____

3. _____

4. _____

5. _____

What can you do today to start working toward those goals?

Item	What I Can Do Today to Achieve the Goal I Want in Five Years

How I Will Achieve My Emotional Goals

Now write specific things you can do to implement the changes you listed.

Within 3 – 6 Months I Will _____

_____

I'm Doing This Because _____

_____

Within 1 – 2 Years I Will _____

_____

I'm Doing This Because _____

_____

Within 3 – 4 Years I Will _____

_____

I'm Doing This Because _____

_____

Putting It All Together

Look at what you like about your emotional life today, and what you've discovered about your wishes, hopes, and dreams for the future. Use these pages to create a story, a poem, an essay, song lyrics, or list describing in words what your emotional future will be like five years from now.

Applying the "Serenity Prayer"

"...grant me the serenity to accept the things I cannot change,

The courage to change the things I can, and

The wisdom to know the difference."

Related to your emotional experience, identify something you cannot change and need to accept.

_____

_____

_____

_____

Describe how you will begin to go about accepting it.

_____

_____

_____

_____

Related to your emotional experience, identify something you can change.

_____

_____

_____

_____

_____

Describe how you will begin to go about changing it.

_____

_____

_____

_____

_____

Describe how you can tell the difference between what you can and cannot change.

_____

_____

_____

_____

_____

The Big Picture

Using whatever technique you prefer (pen/pencil, marker, paints, photos you take yourself or cut from catalogs and magazines—or even a mixed-media combination of all of these), create the portrait of your emotional future here.

MY SPIRITUAL FUTURE

Spirituality—the word represents the essence of comfort and the meaning of life to many people—yet it can be frightening to some or simply meaningless to others. Some people equate spirituality with religion, and for many people, the word "religion" leads to thinking of a particular denomination or of childhood experiences of boring, gloomy, or frightening and interminable worship services conducted in unintelligible languages. If one's feelings about religion are grounded in such experiences, this can create conflict or confusion when the term "spirituality" is mentioned, and the resulting tension can be so great that the urge to ignore or downplay spirituality can cause one to avoid prayer, meditation, or any other "spiritual" practices.

For purposes of this planner, we'll be considering spirituality differently—as a thing apart from religion. It may help to consider that the English word *spirit* comes from the Latin word, *spiritus*, meaning "breath." Thinking of breath, we may think of something we cannot see, but without which we cannot live. So for purposes of this planner, we may define *spirit* as the unseen force that gives us life, or the energy that animates us bodily, mentally, and emotionally—a force that transcends mere physical reality.

Spirituality is thus concerned with the underlying element that binds together all the other parts that make us human, and although it is unseen, and not material or part of the physical world, it is vitally important.

You may never have given your spiritual life much thought, or you may have spent much time, energy, and even money exploring myriad forms of spirituality. Whatever your past experience, let's take a closer look at your spiritual life as it is today, so you can figure out where you are spiritually at this point in your life; for as you have learned by looking at your physical, mental, and emotional states, you need to know where you are before you can move forward.

Spirituality is often thought of as the one element that gives meaning to all the others, and that makes life more than just a collection of days or a physical existence.

Spirituality means different things to different people. Many consider traditional or formal religious practice, including organized worship services, to be important. Others find meaning in exploring a more personal relationship with the world of the spirit. Still others may find their life's purpose expressed in the study of philosophy or in doing good works. Whatever works to build your spiritual life and keep you in spiritual balance is what is right for you.

Spiritual Balance

We too often meet or hear about those who seem obsessed with spirituality—"religious fanatics," some might call them. Some people seem to be completely absorbed in their religion, so much so that they seem to have no time or energy to spend actually living its tenets in this world. Others are almost violently anti-religious—they can't tolerate any mention of prayer, meditation, spirituality, or heaven forbid, God. A balanced spirituality exists somewhere along this continuum.

There are many ways to achieve and maintain a healthy spiritual life. No matter where we begin or what our experiences have been, there is an optimal spiritual state for each of us.

My Spiritual Five-Year Plan: Warming Up

Let's start laying the foundation for your optimal spiritual state by looking at where you are today spiritually.

Begin where you are. Check off each item based on how you feel about it today.

CHECK ONE:	(DISLIKE)	(OKAY)	(LIKE)
My Feelings about Spirituality			
My Knowledge about Spirituality			
My Comfort Level with Spirituality			
My Spiritual Affiliation (if any)			
My Spiritual Practice			
My Spiritual Readings			
My Willingness to Grow Spiritually			

My Five-Year Plan Goals

Five years from now, I'd like (fill in the blank next to the spiritual item listed.)

My Feelings about Spirituality to Be _____

My Knowledge about Spirituality to Be _____

 My Comfort Level with Spirituality to Be _____

My Spiritual Affiliation (if any) to Be _____

My Spiritual Practice to Be _____

My Spiritual Readings to Be _____

My Willingness to Grow Spiritually to Be_____

Whether or not you are happy with your spiritual state today, please list the **top five** things you would like to either change or maintain about your spiritual existence as it is today.

1. _____

2. _____

3. _____

4. _____

5. _____

What can you do today to start changing or to maintain those five items?

Item	What I Can Do Today to Achieve the Goal I Want in Five Years

Thoughts:

Defining Myself without Limiting Myself

My Spiritual Definition

Is there a spiritual practice or system of belief you've always wanted to learn more about? What has held you back from exploring it? Do you have residual fears about learning about spiritual beliefs or practices that are different from those you grew up with? Or do you feel spirituality is the way of weakness? Do you think that since the world of spirituality cannot be seen or touched that it has no value? Please use the lines below to write about your negative attitudes toward spiritual exploration.

_____

_____

_____

_____

_____

In the first column of the chart on the following page, write the spiritual activities and interests you take part in regularly today. If there are none, just leave a blank.

In the second column, write down all the activities you've thought about exploring but just haven't yet tried, for whatever reason. Then try them—visit a church of a different denomination, meditate outdoors, read a spiritual book—whatever seems like a different spiritual practice to you from what you are used to. After you give these new practices a sufficient try, write your reactions in the third column. In column four, write down whether you think you'd like to try it again, and why. There's no need to fill in every column; just do what feels right to you.

COLUMN ONE Spiritual Activity/Practice I Enjoy Regularly (List all)	COLUMN TWO Spiritual Activity/Practice I've Thought about or would Like to Try (List all)	COLUMN THREE What It Was Like	COLUMN FOUR Would I Try It Again? Why or Why Not?

...A Few of My Favorite Things...

Volunteering to help others, advocating for animals or for stewardship of the environment, practicing meditation or yoga, or formal religious worship…all these can be spiritual practices. Do you have a favorite? Use this space to write about it, and why it is a favorite of yours.

Do you have favorite spiritual song/hymn lyrics? Copy them here:

_____

_____

_____

_____

_____

_____

_____

_____

_____

_____

_____

_____

_____

_____

_____

_____

What's your favorite spiritual story (this doesn't have to be from a traditional source; it could be a story about an unexplained event—some might use the word "miracle"—that brought you or someone else closer to your Higher Power; it can be something that happened to you, or something that you heard about that touched your heart.)

_____

_____

_____

_____

_____

_____

_____

_____

_____

_____

_____

_____

_____

_____

_____

_____

_____

_____

_____

_____

_____

_____

_____

_____

_____

_____

_____

_____

_____

_____

_____

_____

_____

_____

_____

_____

_____

Do you have a favorite spiritual author? (Examples might include ancient or contemporary writers and philosophers such as Lao Tzu, C.S. Lewis, Emmett Fox, St. Teresa of Avila, or Deepak Chopra.) Who is your favorite?

_____

_____

_____

_____

Why it this particular author your favorite?

_____

_____

_____

_____

If someone were to quote you on spirituality, what would you want them to say? How would you want others to be helped by your thoughts on spirituality?

_____

_____

_____

_____

_____

What do you want your spiritual legacy to be?

_____

_____

_____

_____

_____

_____

_____

_____

_____

_____

_____

_____

_____

_____

_____

_____

_____

Your Spiritual Wish List

AREAS I KNOW ABOUT	AREAS I'D LIKE TO KNOW ABOUT	WHAT I'LL DO TO LEARN

Spiritual Balance

What exactly does spiritual balance look like? Well, some common characteristics include:

• Keeping a positive attitude.

• Paying attention to and challenging your thoughts.

• Setting achievable goals.

• Being open-minded and willing to try new things.

• Having realistic hope.

Here are some actions others have taken to achieve spiritual balance. Check off those you have tried, and write your experience on the line below.

_____ Nourish your connection to your creative self—sing, build, paint, improve your home, dance, or tell corny jokes.

_____

_____ Practice kindness.

_____

_____ Express your creativity.

_____

_____ Meditate.

_____

_____ Begin or maintain a journal of your thoughts and feelings.

_____

_____ Exercise; walk, dance, move.

_____

_____ Take time to learn about spirituality.

_____

_____ Be good to yourself. Do something you enjoy, every day.

_____

_____ Shake off shame. It kills your spirit and tells you that you are "less than." That feeling keeps you from loving and appreciating YOU— and those around you.

_____

_____ Walk through your fears (even if you have to ask for help). Don't let fear paralyze you.

_____

_____ Be human.

_____

_____ Realize that you have options today. You no longer have to live in the bondage of addiction. You are free today.

_____

Shake Up Your Spiritual Situation

Sometimes we just don't feel connected to our fellowship or to our Higher Power, even though we have been following all our usual practices—and maybe that's it—maybe we need to take a look at our spiritual situation and shake it up, before we can plan to go on with our spiritual journey.

At its core, the spirituality of each human being is unique; there has never been another you, nor will there ever be. You are exactly as you are supposed to be, right here, right now. Your spiritual practices need to be right for you as you are today, and they need to change and grow to fit you as you change and grow.

Take a look at the chart below, and check yes to the items that you recognize in yourself that may be preventing you from growing spiritually—the "Spiritual Stoppers."

SPIRITUAL STOPPER	YES	NO	WHERE I'D LIKE TO BE IN FIVE YEARS
I'm concerned about what others think of me.			
I judge myself by my intentions and excuse my actions.			
I have overextended myself with the pursuit of material things—"shiny objects" like clothes, cars, houses, relationships, etc.			
I seek the approval of others instead of being my own person.			
I try to avoid the disapproval of others at all costs.			

continued on page 134

SPIRITUAL STOPPER	YES	NO	WHERE I'D LIKE TO BE IN FIVE YEARS
I am afraid to speak my mind, whether it's about social issues or what to have for dinner.			
I'm addicted to drama; I love to gossip about others and analyze their actions and motives.			
I seem to have more than my share of crises in my life, and anything can precipitate a crisis, from a misplaced key to an unpaid bill.			
I am glued to the TV and almost feel the characters of my favorite shows are my friends. I get upset if I miss an episode of my favorite show.			
People tell me I overreact to little things. I've heard the words "drama queen" or "drama king" to describe my personality.			
I live in the past, constantly sighing over the way things "used to be" in the "good old days."			
I fear the future, and I resist change.			
I stay in relationships longer than I should because I fear being alone.			
I'm depressed or worried a lot of the time.			

continued on page 135

SPIRITUAL STOPPER	YES	NO	WHERE I'D LIKE TO BE IN FIVE YEARS
I hang around with people who are depressed and worried, too.			
The Internet, TV, shopping, or movies are a way I can escape my depressive thoughts.			
My thoughts wake me up at night.			
I use food, shopping, or other manifestations of addiction to soothe my emotions.			

Based on your answers to the questions above, what conclusions do you draw about your spiritual state? In this exercise, just think about what you have learned about your spirituality today—in the next exercise you'll explore changes you may wish to make.

_____

_____

_____

_____

_____

_____

_____

From Spiritual Stopper to Spiritual Springboard

Think about the changes you'd like to make to your spiritual condition. There are actions you can take today to change the Stoppers you listed into Springboards to where you'd like to be in five years. The example below will get you started—do this every day for several days, and write about your experiences on the lines below. Later you may want to do this exercise in your diary or journal.

Stopper:

"I always 'give in' and do what my partner wants, even if I don't enjoy it, because I fear losing his or her love or having a fight or because I'm really afraid of being left on my own."

Springboard:

*"I practice taking care of myself by saying to my partner, 'You go ahead and enjoy that, but I think I'd rather…read a book…or meditate…or go to a meeting…or **whatever**."* (Just make sure you do something YOU want to do, and don't take part in activities you don't enjoy just because you're afraid of being unloved or being alone.)

_____

_____

_____

_____

_____

_____

_____

_____

Powerful Prayer

Prayer and meditation are powerful spiritual tools of recovery that are recommended in all twelve-step fellowships. Use this page to explore your prayer life today and think about what you want it to be in five years.

If you were to write a prayer, what would your prayer be? Write your own prayer here.

_____

_____

_____

_____

_____

_____

_____

_____

_____

_____

_____

_____

_____

Mighty Meditation

There are many meditation techniques and many books and other resources to help you in your practice of meditation.

Which, if any, have you tried?

_____

_____

_____

_____

_____

Which would you like to try?

_____

_____

_____

_____

_____

If you've been delaying using this powerful tool, here is a simple technique to get you started:

- Select someplace quiet where you are unlikely to be interrupted by other household members.

- Sit or kneel comfortably in any position that doesn't cause you strain. You may sit in a chair if you wish. Put your hands on your thighs, near your knees, or let them lie in your lap. The main thing is to find a position you can comfortably maintain. (Lying down isn't usually recommended, as you may become *too* comfortable.)

- Pick a time when you are unlikely to be interrupted. If you are waiting for a delivery, for example, your meditation may be cut short.

- Tell yourself you will meditate for a set length of time. It needn't be long at first—it's more important that it be a manageable length of time that you can gradually increase. Three to five minutes is perfectly acceptable at first.

- Some people choose a focus word or phrase, called a "mantra," although it's not necessary. This can be the name you call your Higher Power, but doesn't have to be a spiritual word or phrase. You don't even need a focus word at all.

- Close your eyes. This makes it easier to shut out distractions.

- Relax your muscles sequentially from head to feet. As you breathe in, tighten and then loosen your muscles, starting with your forehead, then your jaw, neck, shoulders, and so on. This will release any tension in your muscles, even tension you are unaware of.

- Breathe slowly and naturally, simply noticing your breathing at first, not trying to control it. As you progress, you may try inhaling for four counts, holding the breath for sixteen counts, then exhaling for eight counts. But it is not necessary to do this at first. Just paying attention to your breathing is enough when you are getting started.

- Don't worry about how well or badly you are doing; and don't make a conscious effort to "clear" your mind. Think about your breathing as you inhale and exhale, and if other thoughts intrude, simply notice them and then let them pass through your mind. You can tell yourself something like, "Oh, there's a thought." Just don't follow it. If it's important, it will return later, when you have finished your meditation and can attend to it.

- Continue for the amount of time you told yourself you would. You may open your eyes to check the time. After your meditation, sit quietly for a minute or so, first with your eyes closed and later with your eyes open.

- Remain seated for a moment or two after you open your eyes.

- Plan for a session once or twice a day.

Try this or another favorite meditation technique for a week. Commit to doing it, and then keep that commitment to yourself. Use the blank calendar below to keep a meditation journal for a week. Write down your thoughts and feelings after each session.

Meditation Calendar

SUNDAY	MONDAY	TUESDAY	WEDNESDAY	THURSDAY	FRIDAY	SATURDAY

Where would you like to be in your practice of meditation in 3–6 weeks?

_____

_____

_____

In 3–6 months?

_____

_____

_____

In five years?

_____

_____

_____

Out of Self and into Service

"Faith without works is dead." This axiom is part of twelve-step recovery. As some in the program say, if you're hungry, you can sit in your closet and pray for a cheeseburger, but your Higher Power isn't going to open the door and serve one to you. You have to take appropriate action, and know that your Higher Power will do for you what you cannot do for yourself—not what you *will* not do for yourself.

One of the most powerful spiritual tools of recovery is to be of service to others. This can mean stacking chairs after a meeting, giving a newcomer a ride to a meeting, or standing at the door of a meeting to greet people as they enter. It can also mean performing random acts of kindness, and especially doing good "without getting caught."

Make a "Kindness Diary" for a week. Take time every day to do one kind thing for someone else. Sometimes this can be as simple as holding the door open for a stranger at the mall. It can be letting another driver have the parking spot you are both vying for. Maybe it will be to let your coworker have the last cup of coffee. And if you use the last of the toilet paper, maybe you'll replace the roll. Do these actions sound too silly or simple? That's the point. Service is simple. Do these things mindfully, not to manipulate others into liking you or into liking you *more,* but because you know you are in this world to be of service to God's other kids. Perform service until it's second-nature. It's a spiritual practice that you can grow, beginning today, and continuing into your future, for many more than just five years.

My Kindness Diary

_____

_____

_____

_____

_____

_____

_____

_____

_____

_____

_____

_____

_____

_____

_____

_____

_____

Service

Of course, formal service commitments are a part of twelve-step recovery. Do you currently have a commitment? If not, consider taking one. If you have one, make sure you maintain it. Whether you have one at present or you will take one in the near future, use this calendar to keep a record of your commitment for a month. Record times, dates, and one true thing that happens every time you keep your commitment over the next month.

Service Commitments						
SUNDAY	MONDAY	TUESDAY	WEDNESDAY	THURSDAY	FRIDAY	SATURDAY

What did you learn about yourself and your recovery from your month of service? How will you maintain and grow your service commitments and your informal service to your recovery fellowship over the next five years, starting now?

_____

_____

_____

_____

_____

_____

_____

_____

_____

_____

_____

_____

_____

How I Will Achieve My Spiritual Goals

Now write specific things you can do to implement the changes you listed.

Within 3 – 6 Months I Will _____

_____

I'm Doing This Because _____

_____

Within 1 – 2 Years I Will _____

_____

I'm Doing This Because _____

_____

Within 3 – 4 Years I Will _____

_____

I'm Doing This Because _____

_____

Putting It All Together

Look at what you like about your spiritual life today, and what you've discovered about your wishes, hopes, and dreams for the future. Use these pages to create a story, a poem, an essay, song lyrics, or list describing in words what your spiritual future will be like five years from now.

_____

_____

_____

_____

_____

_____

_____

_____

_____

_____

Applying the "Serenity Prayer"

"...grant me the serenity to accept the things I cannot change,

The courage to change the things I can, and

The wisdom to know the difference."

Related to your spiritual experience, identify something you cannot change and need to accept.

_____

_____

_____

_____

Describe how you will begin to go about accepting it.

_____

_____

_____

_____

Related to your spiritual experience, identify something you can change.

_____

_____

_____

_____

Describe how you will begin to go about changing it.

_____

_____

_____

_____

Describe how you can tell the difference between what you can and cannot change.

_____

_____

_____

_____

The Big Picture

Using whatever technique you prefer (pen/pencil, marker, paints, photos you take yourself or cut from catalogs and magazines—or even a mixed-media combination of all of these), create the portrait of your spiritual future here.

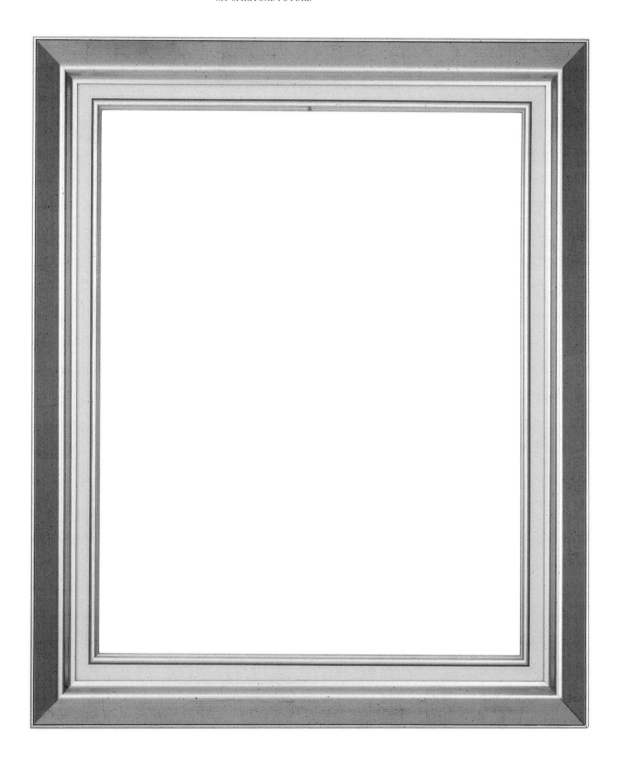

MY FIVE-YEAR RECOVERY PLAN

Congratulations! As you've made your way through this planner, you've done a lot of work toward creating the future you want. But don't stop now just because you are nearing the last page. As you define and work toward your physical, mental, emotional, and spiritual goals, keep this planner close at hand, so that you can check your progress, or maybe even change direction, if in the course of life you find yourself with different goals and dreams than the ones you started your journey with. They're your goals; you can make adjustments as you go along.

Remember that in recovery, we change our behavior to achieve our goals, whereas in our disease, we changed our goals to meet our behavior.

What does your future look like when you achieve your goals? Select one or two top physical, mental, emotional, and spiritual goals, and use the chart below to chart your progress toward achieving them.

My Goals: Year One

HIGHEST PRIORITY GOALS—ONE YEAR FROM NOW	WHAT MY FUTURE LOOKS LIKE WHEN I ACHIEVE THESE GOALS	WHAT I CAN BEGIN TO DO TODAY TO ACHIEVE THESE GOALS

My Goals: Year Two

Start this exercise at the beginning of your second year of working with this planner. At the end of year one, take a look at the goals you've accomplished in your first year, and set your course for year two using the chart below.

HIGHEST PRIORITY GOALS—FOR MY SECOND YEAR	WHAT MY FUTURE LOOKS LIKE WHEN I ACHIEVE THESE GOALS	WHAT I CAN BEGIN TO DO TODAY TO ACHIEVE THESE GOALS

My Goals: Year Three

At the end of year two, take a look at the goals you've accomplished, and set your course for year three in the chart below.

HIGHEST PRIORITY GOALS—FOR MY THIRD YEAR	WHAT MY FUTURE LOOKS LIKE WHEN I ACHIEVE THESE GOALS	WHAT I CAN BEGIN TO DO TODAY TO ACHIEVE THESE GOALS

My Goals: Year Four

At the end of year three, take a look at the goals you've accomplished, and set your course for year four in the chart below.

HIGHEST PRIORITY GOALS—FOR MY FOURTH YEAR	WHAT MY FUTURE LOOKS LIKE WHEN I ACHIEVE THESE GOALS	WHAT I CAN BEGIN TO DO TODAY TO ACHIEVE THESE GOALS

My Goals: Year Five

At the end of year four, take a look at the goals you've accomplished, and set your course for year five in the chart below.

HIGHEST PRIORITY GOALS—FOR MY FIFTH YEAR	WHAT MY FUTURE LOOKS LIKE WHEN I ACHIEVE THESE GOALS	WHAT I CAN BEGIN TO DO TODAY TO ACHIEVE THESE GOALS